DOG BREEDS

Great Danes

by Sara Green

Consultant:
Michael Leuthner, D.V.M.
Petcare Animal Hospital
Madison, Wisc.

BLASTOFF! READERS
4

BELLWETHER MEDIA • MINNEAPOLIS, MN

Note to Librarians, Teachers, and Parents:

Blastoff! Readers are carefully developed by literacy experts and combine standards-based content with developmentally appropriate text.

Level 1 provides the most support through repetition of high-frequency words, light text, predictable sentence patterns, and strong visual support.

Level 2 offers early readers a bit more challenge through varied simple sentences, increased text load, and less repetition of high-frequency words.

Level 3 advances early-fluent readers toward fluency through increased text and concept load, less reliance on visuals, longer sentences, and more literary language.

Level 4 builds reading stamina by providing more text per page, increased use of punctuation, greater variation in sentence patterns, and increasingly challenging vocabulary.

Level 5 encourages children to move from "learning to read" to "reading to learn" by providing even more text, varied writing styles, and less familiar topics.

Whichever book is right for your reader, Blastoff! Readers are the perfect books to build confidence and encourage a love of reading that will last a lifetime!

This edition first published in 2011 by Bellwether Media, Inc.

No part of this publication may be reproduced in whole or in part without written permission of the publisher. For information regarding permission, write to Bellwether Media, Inc., Attention: Permissions Department, 5357 Penn Avenue South, Minneapolis, MN 55419.

Library of Congress Cataloging-in-Publication Data
Green, Sara, 1964–
 Great Danes / by Sara Green.
  p. cm. – (Blastoff! readers. Dog breeds)
 Includes bibliographical references and index.
 Summary: "Simple text and full-color photographs introduce beginning readers to the characteristics of the dog breed Great Danes. Developed by literacy experts for students in kindergarten through third grade"–Provided by publisher.
 ISBN 978-1-60014-566-7 (hardcover : alk. paper)
 1. Great Dane–Juvenile literature. I. Title.
 SF429.G7G74 2011
 636.73–dc22

                                          2010034490

Printed in the United States of America, North Mankato, MN.

010111   1176

Contents

What Are Great Danes?

Great Danes are one of the largest dog **breeds** in the world. People call them "gentle giants" because of their size and friendly nature. Great Danes are members of the **Working Group** of dogs.

Adult Great Danes are 28 to 34 inches (71 to 86 centimeters) tall at the shoulder. They weigh 100 to 160 pounds (45 to 79 kilograms).

mantle

Great Danes look strong and graceful. They have long, muscular necks and large heads with square **muzzles**.

Great Danes have short, shiny **coats**. Their coats can be one solid color, or they can have patterns like **brindle** or **mantle**. The **harlequin** pattern is found only in the Great Dane breed.

harlequin

brindle

! fun fact

A Great Dane with a harlequin coat was the first Great Dane to arrive in the United States. He came in 1857 and was named Prince.

Great Danes are born with long, floppy ears. Many owners like the look of short, pointed ears. They have a **veterinarian** do an operation to **crop** the ears. However, it is becoming more common for owners to leave the ears their natural shape.

History of Great Danes

Irish Wolfhound

The Great Dane is related to the Irish Wolfhound and the Mastiff. Both of these breeds are large and strong.

About 400 years ago in Europe, the two breeds had puppies together. These puppies were the first Great Danes. People used them to hunt **boars**, deer, and other wild animals.

Mastiff

Over time, people stopped using Great Danes as hunting dogs. They started keeping them as guard dogs and **companion dogs** instead.

People began bringing Great Danes to the United States in the middle of the 1800s. The large, friendly dogs soon became popular pets.

Great Danes Today

Great Danes enjoy a variety of activities today. Many owners enter their Great Danes into **dog shows**. At these events, Great Danes compete against each other.

A judge examines each dog's physical features and **gait**. The Great Dane that best represents the breed wins.

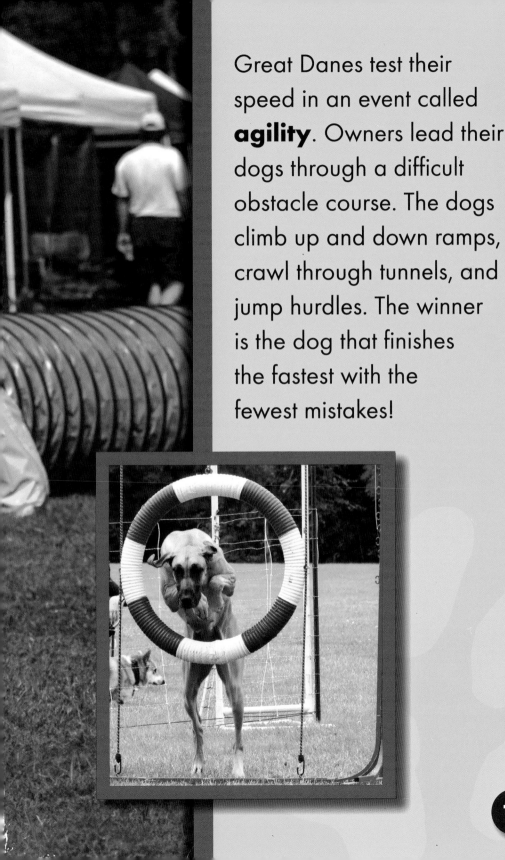

Great Danes test their speed in an event called **agility**. Owners lead their dogs through a difficult obstacle course. The dogs climb up and down ramps, crawl through tunnels, and jump hurdles. The winner is the dog that finishes the fastest with the fewest mistakes!

The gentle nature of Great Danes makes them excellent **therapy dogs**. Some Great Danes visit hospitals, nursing homes, and schools to comfort adults and children.

People with disabilities often use Great Danes as **service dogs**. The tall, strong dogs are especially helpful to people with poor balance. They support people when they walk or stand up.

SERVICE DOG IN TRAINING

Great Danes love to stay home and spend time with their owners. They like to play both outside and inside. They especially enjoy relaxing on the couch with a friend. Do you have room for a Great Dane in your life?

Glossary

agility—a sport where dogs run through a series of obstacles

boars—strong, wild pigs with tusks

breeds—types of dogs

brindle—brown with black stripes or spots

coats—the hair or fur of animals

companion dogs—dogs that provide friendship to people

crop—to cut or shorten a dog's ears

dog shows—competitions where dogs are judged on their physical appearance and gait

gait—a way of walking

harlequin—white with black patches

mantle—black and white with a large patch of solid black

muzzles—the noses, jaws, and mouths of animals

service dogs—dogs that help people with disabilities

therapy dogs—dogs that provide comfort to people

veterinarian—a doctor who takes care of animals

Working Group—a group of dog breeds that do jobs to help humans

To Learn More

AT THE LIBRARY

American Kennel Club. *The Complete Dog Book for Kids*. New York, N.Y.: Howell Book House, 1996.

Fiedler, Julie. *Great Danes*. New York, N.Y.: PowerKids Press, 2006.

Gagne, Tammy. *Great Danes*. Mankato, Minn.: Capstone Press, 2009.

ON THE WEB

Learning more about Great Danes is as easy as 1, 2, 3.

1. Go to www.factsurfer.com.

2. Enter "Great Danes" into the search box.

3. Click the "Surf" button and you will see a list of related Web sites.

With factsurfer.com, finding more information is just a click away.

Index